Ties that Bind

Ties that Bind

Remaining Happy
as a Couple
After the Wedding

Victor M. Parachin

Chalice Press

St. Louis, Missouri

Cover design by Will Hardin

Art Director: Michael Dominguez

Library of Congress Cataloging–in–Publication Data

Parachin, Victor M.
   Ties that bind: remaining happy as a couple after the wedding / by Victor Parachin.
ISBN 0-8272-3630-1
1. Marriage. 2. Interpersonal relations. I. Title.
HQ734.P182 1992   646.7'8   92-329 42

Contents

Introduction

From the twelfth century there is a beautiful legend of love concerning a young and successful London merchant named Gilbert Becket. In 1099 he learned that the Holy City, Jerusalem, had been recaptured from Muslim hands and was now under Christian rule, so he decided to make a pilgrimage to visit the Holy City. Keep in mind that in the twelfth century a trip from England to the Middle East was costly, dangerous, and time-consuming. Preparation for such a trip took more than a year of planning. That included studying Arabic, the language of the Middle East.

Finally, when all was in order, young Gilbert Becket set sail. After sixty days, many of them on stormy seas, Gilbert and his entourage landed at Jaffa

1

(the biblical city of Joppa where Jonah worked). There, Gilbert began the overland trip up to Jerusalem. On the second day of land travel Gilbert, his servant Richard, and the others were captured by a group of Saracens, people of the Muslim faith.

Because Gilbert spoke their language he was presented to the Saracen king. The king was so impressed that this foreigner could speak Arabic that he issued an order not to kill Gilbert because he wanted to keep him as a slave.

By living and serving in the king's household, young Gilbert met the king's beautiful, unmarried daughter. The two young people fell in love: a slave and a princess. In the ensuing months Gilbert gathered up the courage to ask the king for permission to marry his daughter.

Amazingly, the king agreed, perhaps because he saw how happy and how much in love his daughter was with Gilbert. Gradually, the king began to ease up the controls on Gilbert and his servant Richard. One night the two men saw an opportunity to escape. Carefully writing a note to the woman he loved, Gilbert explained his departure and promised: "I will come back for you!" Together, he and Richard slipped out of the palace and into the darkness.

Days turned into weeks and the weeks into months. Gilbert managed to return to England where he busied himself restoring his long-neglected business and renewing old acquaintances. Sadly, he realized it would be difficult if not impossible for him to return to the Middle East and reclaim the woman he loved.

Meanwhile, the young woman began to sense that Gilbert would not be able to return so she decided to find him. Slipping away from her father's home, she began the search. The woman knew very little of life beyond her father's house but Gilbert taught her two words of English: *Gilbert* and *London*. So she made her way to the seaport of Jaffa where she bartered her jewels in exchange for passage to London.

Unable to speak the language and having no idea where Gilbert lived or worked she began her search by moving up one street and down another, saying to people: "Gilbert?" "London?" For days she continued her desperate search.

Providentially, Richard, Gilbert's servant, noticed her in the middle of a crowd because she was wearing her distinctive Middle Eastern clothing. Astonished, he approached her and confirmed that it was indeed the woman Gilbert loved. Richard led her to Gilbert and as soon as their eyes met their love was rekindled.

Of course, they married and had a long, happy life together. Their family included the birth of four children and seventeen grandchildren. Their oldest son, Thomas, later became famous and was known as Thomas Becket, who was martyred as he prayed at Canterbury Cathedral on December 29, 1170.

Love is a power that pulls two people together and enables them to overcome the highest mountain, the deepest valley, and the widest ocean. The writer of the Song of Solomon states: "Many waters cannot quench love,/ neither can floods drown it" (8:7). And in the New Testament, St. Paul declares that love "bears all things, believes all things, hopes all things, endures all things" (1 Corinthians 13:7).

This book is written for those who are about to be married and for those who are married. Behind the book is the premise that people who fall in love want to remain that way. More than anything else in life, they desire to love and be loved by the one they have chosen as a life-mate. The chapters of this book contain solid, practical principles that can lead every man and woman into a lifelong love affair—with each other!

There is no more loving,
friendly and charming
relationship, communion
or company than a good
marriage.
—Martin Luther

Celebrating...
Making Your Wedding the Most Memorable Family Event

♡ On the occasion of his daughter's marriage, one California father turned his estate home into a southern plantation by having millions of magnolia blossoms glued to the trees. In addition, the library, site of the ceremony, was adorned with thousands of orchids and roses.

♡ An urban couple from a Midwest city, who love country, arranged their wedding in a small country church. A wedding quilt was draped across the kneeling bench. The bridesmaids wore dresses in earth-tone colors complete with cream crocheted gloves and straw hats.

♡ A bride and groom in the Northeast created a wedding around the theme *On Golden Pond* by inviting three hundred guests to a 6 a.m. ceremony at the edge of a lake. As the sun rose brilliantly over the water, the couple were pronounced husband and wife.

Whether a wedding is lavish or simple, innovative or traditional, every marriage symbolizes a rite of passage. For that reason weddings become major family festivals. Author and professional hostess, Martha Stewart, in her book entitled *Weddings*, observes:

> A wedding is many things. Foremost it is a rite of passage, an end and a beginning, a fulfillment and a promise. It is one of the three watershed events in the life of humanity and in the company of birth and death, the only one that is voluntary, premeditated, undertaken in full consciousness. Every culture throughout history has commemorated the transition of a human being from one state of life to another and the wedding is anchored at the very heart of civilization.[1]

Every bride and groom wants to have the "perfect" wedding in which family, relatives, and friends gather together in a spirit of unity and joy to celebrate this new beginning. Here are ways to make your wedding the most warm and memorable family celebration ever.

♥ *Have Great Expectations.* Many couples about to be married get nervous and uneasy because they come from blended families. Such couples are concerned about formerly married parents and relatives being together in the same social setting. In her book, *Dear Abby on Planning Your Wedding,* Abigail Van Buren advises couples to be both thoughtful and to have great expectations that the wedding will be a unifying family celebration. She cites this letter from a woman signed "New Bride":

> Dear Abby: I was recently married at a most beautiful wedding. My parents were divorced ten years ago and since that time they had barely spoken a civil word to each other. They both attended my wedding, and were not only polite to each other, they were downright friendly!
>
> Abby, it was the best wedding present either of them could have given me. Please print this in hopes that other divorced couples may see themselves and realize it's possible to put aside their hostilities and bitterness for just one day for the sake of their child. It made my wedding day perfect in every way.[2]

♥ *Assign Honor Roles.* In addition to the bridal party, another way of involving extended family and friends in the actual wedding is to assign honor roles to special friends and relatives. Consider the example of Gail, twenty-five, recently married in Colorado:

> As the wedding date came closer I began to feel swamped with the countless details yet to be taken care of. In particular, I was worried about keeping track of who gave us which gifts. Finally, I asked an elderly aunt if she would "do me the honor of recording gifts as they came in." Not only was she eager to help but was flattered to be more closely involved in the wedding.

Here are other honor roles that can be assigned:

Someone to read scripture or poetry during the ceremony.

Someone to mingle and introduce guests, making certain that no one is left uncomfortably alone.

Someone to help the photographer identify special people for photo opportunities.

Someone to make sure everyone present signs the guest book.

♥ *Mix and Match.* Another creative way to make your wedding warm and memorable is to mix and match people by seating together those who might enjoy each other's company. One new bride says:

> Every wedding provides opportunities to deepen old friendships and establish new ones. My husband and I looked carefully at the seating arrangements for the reception. We put relatives together from different parts of the country who had never met before. Several of them have kept in touch with each other since our wedding. One family has even driven to visit another family from a different state. Both met at our wedding when they were placed together at the same table.

♥ *Be Aware of Intergenerational Differences.* Between the groom's family and that of the bride, there can be as many as three or four generations involved in the celebration. Each family and each generation will have their own ideas about what is and is not appropriate. In order to avoid causing hard feelings, a little advance consideration and modest compromise can result in a big difference.

In her book *The Complete Wedding Planner*, Edith Gilbert makes this suggestion: "It may be difficult for the older generation to adapt to new and different ways of doing things. When the younger generation wishes to be innovative, they may need to consider and respect the feelings of kindly relatives and be open to compromise on unimportant details. It is recommended that friendly communication be developed early on between the families of the bride and groom."[3]

♥ *Include the Disabled.* After finalizing the guest list, look it over carefully to see what special needs people may have. Is there someone confined to a wheelchair who will need special seating arrangements? Is there someone who is blind and may need assistance?

A beautiful incident took place at a wedding in a New York suburb recently. Sharon, the bride, learned that an eleven-year-old niece of her fiancé was born deaf. Sensitively, Sharon sought and found someone who could "sign" the service for the little girl. Sharon said that "following the ceremony that girl's parents came to me with tears in their eyes, thanking me profusely for my kindness to their hearing-impaired daughter."

By doing such careful and thoughtful planning you are assuring yourself of a memorable celebration. It will be one that you and your family will look back upon with great joy and pleasure for many, many years.

[1]Martha Stewart, *Weddings*. Crown Publishers, 1987, p. xii.
[2]Abigail Van Buren, *Dear Abby on Planning Your Wedding*. Andrews & McNeil, 1988, p. 19.
[3]Edith Gilbert, *The Complete Wedding Planner*. Frederick Fell Publishers, 1983, p. 8.

Happiness depends upon
ourselves.

—Aristotle

Connecting...

Ten Skills for a Happy,
Healthy Marriage

On the occasion of his fiftieth wedding anniversary, a man wrote these words to his wife: "After fifty glorious years together I want you to know that there is no mountain tall enough, no valley deep enough, no ocean wide enough to keep me from loving you. Thank you for sharing your life with me."

In spite of the fact that the divorce rate continues to be high, there are many couples, like the one cited above, who know that a good marriage is one of life's greatest pleasures, an enduring source of joy and fulfillment. Here are ten skills that any couple can use to build a healthy, happy marriage.

♥ *Adopt the Sixty-Forty Formula.* Harvey L. Ruben, M.D., is a psychiatrist, happily married for more than twenty years. He and his wife, Diane, have three sons. In his book, *Super Marriage: Overcoming the Predictable Crises of Married Life,* he urges couples not to operate on a "fifty-fifty" approach to marriage but a "sixty-forty" formula.

> In the "sixty-forty" relationship, each of you is willing to be a little more selfless than selfish. You each promise the other that you will try to give sixty percent and expect only forty percent in return. In other words, each of you is trying to please the other, while the other is trying to do exactly the same thing for you. The "sixty-forty" ploy may sound too mechanical but it really works. And I've seen it help couples achieve success in negotiating the most difficult passages.[1]

♥ *Offer the Gift of Empathy.* A common biblical theme is for Christians to feel what another person is feeling, to walk in that person's shoes. Here are some examples: "Be happy with those who are happy, weep with those who weep" (Romans 12:15 TEV). "Help carry one another's burdens" (Galatians 6:2 TEV). "Remember those who are suffering, as though you were suffering as they are" (Hebrews 13:3b TEV).

What these verses indicate for married couples is that they should offer each other the gift of empathy. Rather than becoming annoyed by the behavior of a spouse and passing harsh judgments, we should try to understand what he or she is experiencing by pausing to ask ourselves: What kind of day has he had? What is behind her anger? What is it like to be him right now? What has she experienced to make her react this way?

♥ *Pull Together.* Every couple will experience times of stress and crisis. Such life crises run the gamut: unemployment, a grim medical diagnosis, disability, death of a loved one. During difficult times healthy couples unite rather than pull apart. John DeFrain, professor in the department of human development and the family at the University of Nebraska and co-author of *Secrets of Strong Families,* says:

> Members of strong families unite to face the challenges of a crisis. The question they ask is not, "What needs to be done?" Sometimes the task is enormous. Nobody could do it alone. The question is, "What can I do?" Strong family members focus on the small things they can do as individuals to help. No individual feels total responsibility for the problem. Nobody carries the load alone. They all shoulder it together.[2]

♥ *Be Together.* One of the major issues facing most couples today is the lack of discretionary time. Most people find their free time evaporates each week. Yet, the busiest and happiest couples make time to be together.

One example is Louis and Ginger Sullivan. As secretary of Health and Human Services in the Bush administration, Dr. Sullivan had an extremely full and hectic schedule. His workday often extended into fourteen hours. Nevertheless, his relationship to his wife continued to be a priority.

> Despite my busy schedule as a Cabinet officer, I am very committed to spending time with my wife and children. My wife Ginger and I set aside time each morning for a 45-minute walk.

This gives us a chance to talk, share thoughts, express appreciation for each other and get some exercise.[3]

♥ *Make Yourself Available.* A relationship must never be taken for granted. Happy couples are intentional about remaining connected. Kevin and Marilyn Ryan, a married couple who have co-authored the book *Making a Marriage,* offer this observation about their own marriage:

When we get in trouble with one another, it's often because we haven't been giving one another the time that a marriage demands. We quietly slip into our own life and block the other out. We need to remind ourselves consciously that to build anything as elusive and fluid as a good marriage takes time, and it takes time on a regular basis.[4]

♥ *Be Liberal with Praise.* In contemporary society people are constantly confronted with criticism from employers, educators, even friends. As a result many people struggle with self-doubt. In strong marriages partners know how to praise and affirm each other. They are guided by this advice from the apostle Paul: "Fill your minds with those things that are good and that deserve praise: things that are true, noble, right, pure, lovely, and honorable" (Philippians 4:8 TEV).

♥ *Be Conservative with Criticism.* Before offering any word of criticism, consider this advice from psychologist Dr. James Dobson: "The right to criticize must be earned, even if the advice is constructive in nature. Before you are entitled to tinker with another person's self-esteem, you are obligated first to demonstrate your respect for him (or her) as a person."[5]

♥ *Tap Spiritual Resources.* Connected couples identify a common spiritual life as an important bonding aspect of their marriages. One woman, thirty-seven, married for fifteen years, says: "I can't imagine sharing my life with a husband who didn't believe in God and who did not attend worship with me. It would be like living with an alien. My husband and I have always been active in our church. We attend worship services weekly as a family; we sit together. It is an important source of renewal for all of us."

♥ *Renew and Restore.* Couples who remain in love are careful about renewing and restoring themselves physically and emotionally. "About twice a year we leave our children with their grandparents for a long weekend," says one husband. "Then, my wife and I check into a downtown hotel where we sleep late, lounge around the pool and do some leisurely browsing in downtown shops. This 'pause' in our hectic schedules is always a source of renewal for us; a time when we reconnect."

♥ *Show Your Love.* Happy couples know how to show love and they do so frequently and consistently. Along with saying "I love you" these couples back their words up with tangible expressions of love: gifts of flowers, jewelry, clothing, tickets to concerts, trips, weekend escapes. Their creative ways of demonstrating love are endless but all designed with one goal: to shower their mates with symbols of their love and affection.

After all is said and done, perhaps this advice from Dr. Louis W. Sullivan is appropriate for every couple: "There may be days when you feel like calling it quits. Don't give up! If you make time for each other, communicate, encourage and appreciate each other, you will be well on your way to building a happy marriage that will last a lifetime."

[1]Harvey Ruben, *Super Marriage: Overcoming the Predictable Crises of Married Life*. Bantam Books, 1986, p. 21.

[2]Nick Stinnett and John DeFrain, *Secrets of Strong Families*. Little, Brown & Co., 1985, p. 128.

[3]Louis Sullivan, "On the Eve of Your Marriage." *Elegant Bride*, Feb/Mar 1992, p. 220.

[4]Kevin and Marilyn Ryan, *Making a Marriage*. St. Martin's Press, 1982, p. 43.

[5]James Dobson, *What Wives Wish Their Husbands Knew About Women*. Living Books, 1985, p. 161.

What is a friend?
A single soul dwelling in
two bodies.
　　　　　—Aristotle

3

Caring...

How to Stay Friends with Your Spouse After You Say "I Do"

In 1966 Rick was an unmarried serviceman stationed in Vietnam. Through the mail he received a copy of his hometown newspaper and saw the graduation picture of Jerri, a senior from his old high school.

"Although I never met her, the picture did something for me so I cut it out and put it in my wallet. During my tour of duty I would look at Jerri's picture and think about meeting her. It gave me something to look forward to," he says.

When he was discharged he tracked Jerri down, who was then in college, and asked her out. She accepted and later that year they were married.

Soon they will celebrate nearly twenty-five years together. When asked about their relationship, Jerri replied enthusiastically:

"Rick is not just my husband and lover, he's also my best friend!"

Every good marriage has as its foundation friendship between husband and wife. The simple reality that a partner is, in fact, a best friend empowers a husband and wife to deal creatively with every change and challenge that comes their way.

It doesn't matter if you are about to be married, are recently married or, like Rick and Jerri, have been married several years, it is possible to have your spouse as your best friend. Here are strategies for maintaining a friendship with your spouse after you say "I do."

♥ *Practice Unconditional Love and Acceptance.* The most secure marriages and the most satisfying relationships have, at their core, an understanding of unconditional love and acceptance. For example, Richard Selzer, a surgeon and author of *Mortal Lessons*, tells of being present when a husband visited his young wife shortly after Selzer performed surgery to her face.

Unfortunately, in order to remove a tumor on her cheek, Selzer accidently severed a tiny, hair-thin nerve that controlled the muscles of her mouth. The woman could no longer smile properly and one side of her mouth drooped. She was nervous about her husband's reaction since she knew that the damage was permanent.

When her husband entered the room, he simply looked at his wife and said: "I like it. It is kind of cute." Then he bent down to "kiss her crooked mouth," Selzer reports. "I am so close I can see how he twists his own lips to accommodate to hers, to show her that their kiss still works."[1]

♥ *Bring out the Lover in Your Spouse.* One of the major disappointments for many married couples is the decline of intimacy and sexuality. Hectic schedules, the arrival of children, and work problems can squeeze out time and energy for intimacy. Yet, couples who have close relationships know that frequent sexual connecting is important and therefore they give it priority.

Sherry is an executive producer in the Chicago area. She has been married fifteen years, has three young children, and works a fifty-five hour week in the emotionally demanding field of video production.

In spite of time restraints and emotional pressure on her, she regularly lets her husband know that sexuality is important to her. One of her ways to do this occurs around the time of their anniversary. Every year as their wedding date approaches she carefully selects and buys the most seductive lingerie she can find. She says, "I've done that every year for the fifteen years of our marriage. I do it for him and I do for myself. It's a reminder to both of us that we love and want each other."

♥ *Demonstrate Your Love.* People who are truly in love with each other demonstrate their love in natural, spontaneous ways. It is almost second nature for them to do this. A wonderful example comes from an ancient story in the Middle East. At the time, Cyrus was the most powerful ruler in the area. His name is cited in the Old Testament book of Isaiah.

During his reign there was a local chieftain named Caligula (not related to a later Roman ruler). Caligula's land bordered the southern tip of Cyrus' kingdom. There was a war over the territory between the armies of Cyrus and Caligula. Cyrus defeated Caligula in battle and, in keeping with the rules of war at that time, Caligula and his wife were summoned before King Cyrus to receive death sentences.

Ordinarily, the sentencing was automatic. However, Cyrus was impressed by Caligula who stood before him tall, strong, courageous, and dignified. So Cyrus began to question him:

"Caligula, what would you do if I spared your life?"

"Sir, I would return to my home with gratitude and remain for the rest of my life your obedient servant," Caligula responded.

"And what would you do if I spared your wife?"

"Sir, if you would do that I would gladly die for you," Caligula responded again.

So impressed was Cyrus that he required of Caligula only that he give an oath of allegiance to the king. Then he sent Caligula and his wife away, free citizens.

Once they were home, Caligula and his wife were talking. Caligula said to her:

"Did you notice the beautiful marble in the king's palace?"

"I didn't see it," she answered.

"Then, did you see the magnificent tapestries on the walls of the palace?" he asked.

"No, I didn't see them," she replied.

"Well, what did you see the day we stood before the king in his opulent palace?"

"I saw only the face of one who said he would die for me," was her memorable reply.

For all of us there are large and small ways to show our love. Every expression of love further bonds the relationship, assuring both partners of mutual lifelong satisfaction.

♥ *Be Supportive.* Every person goes through periods of personal and professional difficulty. During those times people feel lonely and vulnerable and need extra support to get them through.

Opera singer Beverly Sills is regarded as the finest soprano the United States has ever produced. She began her singing career on radio in 1932 singing on *Uncle Bob's Rainbow House*. From radio she moved on to sing first with the Philadelphia Civic Opera and then the New York City Opera. In 1956 she married Peter Greenough, whose family owned the *Plain Dealer*, a Cleveland newspaper.

Initially, the marriage meant living in Cleveland. "I hated Cleveland," Sills remembers. "Bad for my marriage, bad for my career." Fortunately for both Beverly and Peter, their family paper was sold, allowing the couple to move back East where Sills continued her operatic career.

Their marriage produced two children who brought them great joy. However, that joy was shattered when the couple learned that their daughter was deaf. That would be a terrible blow to any parent, but especially Beverly and Peter for whom music and the ability to hear it was a vital aspect of their lives.

Adding to that tragedy was the fact they discovered their second child, a son, was autistic. Beverly Sills speaks tenderly and warmly of her husband's steady support for her when she was devastated by the double trials of her children's conditions. She went into a deep depression and could no longer sing. When asked how she managed to work her way through that struggle, she replied:

"We were living in Boston and Peter, my husband, gave me a gift of 52 round-trip tickets from Boston to New York. It forced me to go back each week to study, to practice, to find again the discipline I needed. Those 52 round-trip tickets saved me."[2]

♥ *Be Loyal.* Loyalty is an essential ingredient for any successful relationship. Love flourishes in an environment where couples maintain steadfast loyalty to each other in good times as well as bad times.

An example is that of Diane, a woman whose husband lost his job and his self-confidence. He says:

> Because of the abrupt way I was fired, my colleagues were afraid to be in contact with me, believing they too could lose their jobs just by talking to me. In the end, the only person who stood by me and kept coaxing me to continue looking for something better was my wife Diane. I now have a much better position, but without her support I don't think I could have made it.

The reason loyalty deepens the bond between two people is because loyalty always conveys total acceptance. A beautiful incident took place in the lives of a couple, Carol and Fred, when Fred finally summoned the courage to ask his boss for a raise.

He told his wife, Carol, what he intended to do at work that morning. Late in the afternoon, when an opportune moment arrived, Fred approached his employer. To his amazement and delight, his boss agreed and gave him a substantial raise.

Rushing home after work, Fred arrived home to find a beautiful table set with their finest china. Candles were lighted. His wife had prepared to celebrate. Naturally, Fred concluded someone from the office had called Carol and informed her of the good news.

Finding his wife in the kitchen, he went ahead and shared his joy with her. They embraced, kissed, then sat down to a wonderful meal. Next to his place he found a beautiful handwritten note that read: "I knew you'd get the raise! These things will tell you how much I love you."

Later, when Fred's wife rose to bring dessert from the kitchen, he noticed that a second card had fallen from her pocket. Picking it off the floor, he was astonished to read:

"Don't worry about not getting the raise. You deserve it anyway! These things will tell you how much I love you."

That kind of loyalty and devotion assures both Fred and Carol of a lifelong, happy marriage.

♥ *Make the Relationship a Priority.* It is amazing how many spouses take their partner for granted soon after they are married. Anne Mayer, author of *How to Stay Lovers While Raising Your Children,* writes: "After couples have been married for a while, spouses often get the notion that the hunt is over. They stop trying to make themselves attractive and stimulating."[3]

Couples who have fulfilling marriages know better. Throughout the entire marriage they act in ways that show the relationship is a high priority. One woman, a mother of four children, says:

"I take nothing for granted in our relationship. I know that initially my husband was attracted to me by my appearance. So, I continue to dress well and constantly work at improving my wardrobe. I never let go of my efforts to be appealing for my husband."

In the nineteenth century poet Percy Bysshe Shelley once wrote that a friend is "a smile among dark frowns, a gentle tone among rude voices, a beloved light, a solitude, a refuge, a delight." That friend can and should be your spouse. It is a friendship well worth nurturing.

[1] Richard Selzer, *Mortal Lessons: Notes on the Art of Surgery.* Simon & Schuster, 1987, p. 17.

[2] Beverly Sills, cited in *Parade*, Nov. 5, 1989, p. 30.

[3] Anne Mayer, *How to Stay Lovers While Raising Your Children*. Price Stearn Sloan Inc., 1990, p. 133.

Communicating...

Simple Secrets for Healthy Communications

From a West African tribe comes a powerful story about the importance of communication. The people of that tribe tell the legend of the Sky Maiden. Long ago their ancestors observed that their cattle gave less milk then they used to.

It was disturbing because no one in the tribe knew what the problem was.

One of the young men volunteered to stay up all night watching the cattle to see if he could determine what was happening. After hiding behind some bushes for several hours he saw something extraordinary take place in the middle of the night. A beautiful young woman rode a moonbeam down from heaven to earth. She carried a large silver pail.

25

Once on the ground she began to milk the cows. When her pail was full she quickly climbed the moonbeam back up into the sky. The young observer could not believe what he had just witnessed.

So, the next night he set a trap where the cows were kept. When the woman of astonishing beauty came down her moonbeam to milk the cows, he sprang the trap and caught her.

"Who are you?" he demanded.

"I am a Sky Maiden, a member of a tribe that lives in the sky. We have no food of our own and it is my job to come down to earth each evening to find food for my people," she explained.

Then the Sky Maiden pleaded with the young man to release her from the net. In turn she promised to do anything he asked. The man agreed to let her go, but only if she would marry him.

"I will marry you but first you must let me go home for three days to prepare myself. Then I will return and be your wife," she said.

The man released her and three days later the Sky Maiden returned. She brought along a large box and explained:

"I will be your wife and make you very happy, but you must promise me never to look inside this box."

For several weeks they were very happy together. Then one day when his wife was away, the man, overcome with curiosity, opened the box. Stunned, he saw there was nothing in it. When his wife returned she saw her husband look strangely at her.

"You looked in the box, didn't you? I can no longer live with you," she told him.

"Why?" the man asked. "What is so terrible about my peeking into an empty box?"

"I'm not leaving you because you opened the box. I

thought you would sooner or later. I am leaving you because you said it was empty. It wasn't empty; it was full of sky.

"It contained the light and the air and the smells of my home in the sky. When I went home for the last time, I filled that box with everything that was most precious to me to remind me of where I came from. *How can I be your wife if what is most precious to me is emptiness to you?*"

Sadly, that legend represents too many relationships today where what is precious, important, and valued by one is worthless, empty, and minimized by the other. In order for this gap never to occur between a husband and wife, it is vital and crucial for there to be continuous communication.

Yet, when people become too busy, sometimes the simple task of conversation gets lost in the hectic schedule. For example, a psychologist recently measured the amount of conversation that occurs between a husband and wife during a one week period of time. To ensure accuracy, the researcher strapped portable electronic microphones to husbands and wives. That way he could measure every word exchanged between couples. He was able to time each conversation: moments traveling in the car, requests to pass the cream, simple announcements that a package had arrived.

He determined there are 168 hours in a week, 10,080 minutes. The psychologist was shocked to discover that the average couple spent a mere seventeen minutes per week in conversation.

How different from the early stages of dating when a man and a woman can spend hours at a time just talking. Yet, for love to deepen and grow spouses must continue to speak and listen to each other. Every couple will experience differences of opinion and even more serious conflicts. These can quickly be cleared up by open, honest talk. Here are several simple secrets for healthy communication.

♥ *Be Open.* While negative or critical comments about ourselves are difficult to hear, a positive resolution is more likely to emerge if we work at being open. This advice from actor Carroll O'Connor is an excellent starting point for effective communication.

> Establish a policy of taking all criticism as friendly. Once you insist to yourself that the other person is well-intentioned, you'll get value from legitimate criticism, if there's any there to get, and you won't be bothered by the rest. When you concede a critic's good will, you disarm an attacker and encourage an ally.[1]

♥ *Count to Ten.* Everyone should recall that words can injure or inspire, hurt or heal. So many regrets and deeper complications can be avoided by pausing and thinking before anything is spoken.

This advice is offered by Alanston B. Houghton, author of *Partners in Love.* He says:

> Before you say anything, think it through—bite your tongue—count to ten. You want to be heard by your partner. Therefore, present your views calmly and carefully. A few seconds of caution can save hours of pain. Real intimacy, which I think is the bedrock of any successful marriage partnership, is largely due to two people loving each other enough and trusting each other enough to feel safe enough to share deep, deep feelings without fear of criticism, rejections or loss of love.[2]

♥ *Focus on Feelings, Not Faults.* Healthy communication and a fair fight will take place when accusations are avoided. It is much healthier (and safer) when the conversation is about feelings rather than blame.

In his book, *The Friendship Factor,* therapist Alan McGinnis explains: "If a wife says to her husband, 'You never pay any attention to me anymore,' it is almost certain to wave a red flag. We always react [negatively] when someone says, 'You never...' and 'you always....'"

McGinnis suggests a better response from the wife would be: "'You know, I'm really feeling lonely and neglected these days.' She is saying the same thing as 'you never pay any attention to me anymore,' but note the difference: She's not accusing him of anything. She's just telling what she's feeling."[3]

♥ *Speak in Nonthreatening Ways.* Counselors urge couples to move from "offensive" to "nonoffensive" ways of communication. The following statements are considered threatening or offensive: "You did this to me!" "It's entirely your fault." "You always stand in my way." Such statements only provoke the other person to respond angrily and defensively.

Therapists suggest transforming such sentences into nonthreatening statements that open the way for healthy discussion. Here are some more positive, nonthreatening ways of responding to issues: "I feel hurt when you act that way." "Have you ever considered?..." "You may not realize this but I get upset when you say that." These kinds of sentences invite the other person to listen and respond with sensitivity.

Dr. Zev Wanderer and Erika Fabian, in their book *Making Love Work*, explain:

If your mate does something that truly up-sets you, ask him or her: "I wonder how you would feel if I had done this?" But don't imply with your question: "You're so exasperating, that even you couldn't handle it!" If that's the way you ask your mate, you'll get into a worse battle. So be careful to use the tone of voice that will indicate genuine inquiry, not an accusation.[4]

♥ *Don't Criticize or Judge.* People always find criticism painful even if it is valid. And no one likes to be judged. Criticism and judgment escalate tensions while weakening relationships. Strong marriages and healthy communication result when partners frame their needs and expectations in positive ways.

Barbara Russell Chesser, author of *21 Myths That Can Wreck Your Marriage: How a Couple Can Avoid Head-on Collisions,* states: "Unfortunately, many couples rarely speak to each other except when something is wrong....Marriages thrive when spouses affirm one another's strengths and minimize weaknesses. Or as philosopher William James expressed it, 'The art of being wise is the art of knowing what to overlook.'"[5]

♥ *Please Touch.* Dr. McGinnis says: "If you want to get closer to those around you, be aware of the power of communication which you hold in your hands. In my work I am sometimes at a loss to know what to say in the face of the complex problems presented by patients. Sometimes I impulsively rise from my chair and put my hand on the patient's arm in an attempt to convey how deeply I feel."[6]

The fact is that a touch, embrace, or hug provides encouragement and comfort while conveying tenderness and understanding.

An example is that of Martha, who came home to her husband, Mark, in tears after work. "I blurted out to Mark how badly I had been treated that day by my boss. Mark was wonderful. He just let me talk and talk and talk without interrupting. When I was through with my sad tale of woe he just hugged me tightly. Again, no words were spoken, yet his touch told me how much he loved me and felt for me."

♥ *Listen with the Heart.* When someone is speaking, it is important to hear not only the words but to recognize the feelings behind the words. Professional therapists do this all the time. It is called listening with the "third ear."

One man speaks eloquently about his wife: "When I pour out my heart she really listens as I talk. But more than just listening, she hears in the tone of my voice what my words do not say. My wife is a master listener because she catches the feelings buried in the words."

♥ *Practice the Art of Affirmation.* Communication flourishes and marriages thrive when couples lavish praise upon each other. Pioneer American psychologist, William James, observed: "The deepest principle in human nature is the craving to be appreciated." Of course, to be effective, such affirmation must be sincere and honest. False flattery is counterproductive. One couple, happily married for nearly twenty years, make it a habit to offer at least one compliment every day.

♥   *Think Ahead.* If something in your partner needs correcting, prepare your thoughts and words in advance. Whenever you have to assert yourself, improvising as you are speaking can lead to disaster.

Consider Paula, who has been married to James for three years. "We get along fabulously," she says. "However, there are times of friction between us. We both operate on the rule that it is wise to think before speaking. So, before I criticize James about anything, I try to put just the right words and sentences together."

♥ *Always Express Your Love.* When there is a difference of opinion over a matter and a heated exchange has taken place, always reassure your spouse of your love. One woman is highly skilled in this art. "Honey, I love you," she said, "but I hate it when you leave your clothes all over the floor." Then she leaned forward and gave him a light kiss on the cheek. The end result: he picks up his clothing more often, she sleeps better, and the bedroom is tidier.

And if you get discouraged, recall the truth in this statement by St. Jerome, a theologian of the fourth century: "He who lives without quarreling is a bachelor." Although everyone in a relationship will experience disagreement and conflict, by adapting these simple strategies any friendship will remain healthy, joyful, and a great source of fulfillment.

[1]Carroll O'Connor, cited in Walter Anderson, *Courage Is a Three-Letter Word.* Random House, 1988, p. 203.

[2]Alanston Houghton, *Partners in Love: Ingredients for a Deep and Lively Marriage.* Walker & Co., 1988, p. 42.

[3]Alan McGinnis, *The Friendship Factor.* Augsburg, 1979, p. 104.

[4]Zev Wanderer and Erika Fabian, *Making Love Work.* Putnam & Sons, 1979, p. 124.

[5]Barbara Russell Chesser, *21 Myths That Can Wreck Your Marriage: How a Couple Can Avoid Head-on Collisions.* Word Inc., 1990, p. 27.

[6]McGinnis, *The Friendship Factor,* p. 84.

My own view, for what it's worth, is that sexuality is lovely, there cannot be too much of it.
—Paul Goodman

Loving...
The Ingredients for Great Married Sex

Cynthia, married four years, expresses frustration over her relationship with her husband, Larry, saying: "He's become a night person and I've always been a morning person. By 10 p.m. I'm exhausted and getting ready to sleep. But Larry is just beginning to settle into a chair where he will spend the next two or three hours watching television. This difference is causing havoc with our sex life. We rarely connect anymore. Gone are the days when sex was a wonderful priority and a source of great closeness between us."

Her concern is reflected in a recent study. Researchers looked at sexual patterns in newlyweds and discovered that after just one year of marriage, sexual activity between husbands and wives is reduced by 50 percent.

Furthermore, advice columnist Ann Landers, after hearing from thousands of people, has made this observation: "Women complain about sex more often than men. Their gripes fall into two major categories: (1) not enough. (2) too much."[1]

While most husbands and wives continue to believe that sex is very important to a good marriage, finding the time and establishing mutually comfortable patterns is difficult to do. Just as sexuality can be a great source of fulfillment, it can also be a great source of frustration. Therefore, the matter of sexual intimacy is not something to be taken for granted. Here are key ingredients that, when put together, lead to great married sex.

♥   *Make Sex a Priority.* Because life can become filled and crowded with all sorts of issues and events, it is in the vital interest of every couple to place a premium on maintaining sexual intimacy. This advice is strongly recommended by sex therapist Helen Singer Kaplan, who says:

> One way to avoid shortchanging your relationship is to place a higher priority on sex. *Don't* put lovemaking at the bottom of your list, after the 11 o'clock news. *Do* schedule a regular weekly date with your husband—to go out to dinner or simply spend an evening at home alone together. Try not to let anything prevent you from keeping this date.[2]

Sexually compatible and happy couples are those who make sex a common goal. They understand the importance of a sexual bond and work together to have it happen often.

♥ *Practice the "Three Rs."* People are constantly growing, maturing, evolving, and changing. Nothing about human beings remains the same for any length of time. That is also true of sexual feelings. Therefore it is important for couples to practice the "Three Rs": *renegotiating* their desires, *reinterpreting* their partner's needs, and *reinventing* their sexuality together.

Consider Judy and David, both in their early thirties and married eight years. Judy admits that their lovemaking has waned and become "too predictable." After finally gathering up her courage she spoke with David about making some sexual changes together.

> I realized before we were married I had very limited sexual experience. Now after eight years of marriage my sexual appetite had expanded considerably. I suggested we try to do things differently and try some experimenting. David was wonderfully responsive to my thoughts. Initially he was a little reluctant, I think, but now he's extremely enthusiastic about acting out on our fantasies.

♥ *Express and Explore Fantasies.* Fantasizing is normal says Daniel Barlow, director of the sexuality research program at the State University of New York in Albany. His research indicates the average person has six or seven sexual fantasies each day, while some report having up to forty such fantasies daily. Consider also this information from Miriam Arond and Samuel L. Pauker, who surveyed two thousand newly married couples. Of the 346 who responded to their questionnaire, 86 percent reported having sexual fantasies.

In their book, *The First Year of Marriage: What to Expect, What to Accept, and What You Can Change,* Arond and Pauker conclude fantasies play a "positive role" in marriage because they bring spouses together, increase sexual pleasure, and offer clues to a spouse's sexual needs and desires.[3]

As a result, therapists recommend that partners share their fantasies with each other. Alexandra Penney, author of *How to Make Love to Each Other,* says: "Couples who enjoy acting out or talking about their fantasies very often report a special, exhilarating sense of playfulness in their relationships....The basis of fantasy is imagination, and for many couples, the freedom to use their imaginations freely can be one of the most liberating, exciting aspects of lovemaking. Imagination can spark romance and rekindle it."[4]

Expressing and exploring fantasy can start off in small ways and lead to larger, more complete acts. "If you're interested in exploring your imagination you can simply indulge yourselves in mildly erotic daydreams," says Penney, "or you can go all the way to performing the most intricate and detailed scenarios complete with real props and scripts."

♥ *Communicate and Illustrate.* It is always a huge mistake to complain about sex, especially during lovemaking. And it is always better to communicate and illustrate desires in kind and gentle ways. Dr. Kaplan advises:

> Remember that there are tactful ways of asking your partner to give you what you want without discouraging him and sabotaging sex. Suppose, for example, you're dissatisfied because your husband consistently climaxes very rapidly. This is one sexual problem that's

easily cured. But don't bring it up while you're making love.

Instead, wait for an appropriate moment to tell him you love him. You might say, "I think the two of us could have a better sex life. Maybe we would both have more fun if you could last longer. I've heard there are ways to help you do this. How do you feel about that?" Rather than criticizing him, you are letting him know that you care about him and are committed to improving your love life together.[5]

♥   *Provide Positive Feedback.* Most couples find sex difficult to talk about because it reveals our deepest, most intimate self. Yet, there are ways to talk about our sexual needs that are helpful, not harmful. Here are some positive approaches to the delicate issue of sexuality:

Express Appreciation. This can be done before sex ("I like that idea!"); during sex ("I love it when you do this"); and after the act ("It really felt good when you...").

Show Your Mate. Sometimes it's easier and quicker to simply show your partner what would feel good. Take her hand or guide him to do things that enhance pleasure.

Be Tactful. Never be judgmental or make harsh accusations about a sexual relationship. Don't use unkind sentences like these: "You're so selfish in bed." "You never do what I want." "All you're concerned about is your orgasm." Such statements are always counterproductive.

Turn Suggestions into Questions. This is always less threatening. For example, "Wouldn't it be more pleasurable to spend more time exploring each other?" "Could we plan something special for later today?" "How would it be if we tried something really different tonight?"

♥ *Don't Hesitate—Initiate!* Avoid falling into a pattern where the same person, usually the male, is always the one to initiate lovemaking. When both partners share responsibility for a satisfying sex life neither one will be left feeling angry because they want it more than the other, nor will partners feel frustrated because they there is not enough sexual contact in the relationship. Aim for equality in the bedroom.

Consider the plight of Fred, married to Carol. Fred explains:

> During the first two years of our marriage I always initiated sex. Increasingly, I was developing self-doubts about myself and our sex life because I seemed to be the one always wanting it. Finally, we talked about it. Carol assured me she enjoyed lovemaking with me but was timid about initiation. However, I told her that I would feel more physically attractive and desirable if she would initiate periodically. To her credit, she understood and initiates sex more often. As a result, we're both more satisfied.

♥ *Be Realistic.* While it is important to plan and prioritize for sexuality, every couple should have realistic expectations. There will be times when lovemaking is highly intense and satisfying. However, there will be other occasions when sexual satisfaction is only moderate. Alexandra Penney wisely advises:

You are not going to have a transcendent experience every time you make love. If you feel that the fireworks should go off every time, you're both going to have to fake a lot. And faking is precisely the opposite of what intimacy is all about. Sexual desire, sexual passion, sexual enthusiasm, like other emotions, ebb and flow. Even in the closest, most intense relationships, lovemaking will have its ups and downs.[6]

While these techniques will help any couple, the basis for sexual intimacy should be a deep and abiding love for each other. Steve Carter and Julia Sokol interviewed scores of happily married couples for their book, *What Really Happens in Bed*. They were surprised by what they discovered:

"At the core of the happy marriage seems to be something quite special: love. We were impressed and often inspired by the way in which so many happily married men and women voluntarily expressed the strength and quality of love they feel for their partners."

Among the people who consider their marriages successful, both the men and women were consistent in telling Carter and Sokol that "love, not lust, is the glue that keeps a relationship together; love, not lust, is what motivates couples to work on their problems and accept or overlook those things that cannot be changed. Love, not lust, is what created stability, productivity and marital longevity."[7]

[1]Ann Landers, cited in *Cosmopolitan*, December 1991, p. 124.

[2]Helen Singer Kaplan, "Keep Your Marriage Sexy: 10 Mistakes to Avoid." *Redbook*, April 1989, p. 166.

[3]Miriam Arond and Samuel Pauker, *The First Year of Marriage: What to Expect, What to Accept, and What You Can Change.* Warner Books, 1987, p. 247.

[4]Alexandra Penney, *How to Make Love to Each Other*. Berkeley Books, 1982, p. 151.

[5]Kaplan, "Keep Your Marriage Sexy: 10 Mistakes to Avoid," p. 166.

[6]Penney, *How to Make Love to Each Other,* p. 116.

[7]Steve Carter and Julia Sokol, *What Really Happens in Bed: A Demystification of Sex*. M. Evans & Co., 1989, p. 88.

Money has a power above
The stars and fate,
To manage love.
　　　　—Samuel Butler

ℱinancing...
Managing Money Together Without a Battle

Although Greg and Karen have been married three years and feel their marriage is solid, they are both concerned that battles over money are escalating. "We're fighting more and more about how our money is spent," she admits.

Because they each work full time their income exceeds their expenses. Yet they accuse each other of spending money carelessly. "Karen became extremely upset when I told her I wanted to buy a new car. What I'm driving now is no longer reliable," he says. "Greg flatly vetoed my plans to upgrade and purchase a new computer. I'm a free-lance writer and need it for my work," Karen says angrily.

Most marriage counselors will not be surprised by the tension that exists between Karen and Greg. Money is the major cause of disagreement between spouses. In their book, *The First Year of Marriage,* authors Miriam Arond and Samuel L. Pauker surveyed hundreds of newly married couples. According to their survey money is the leading cause of argument among newlyweds. Sixty-three percent of the couples polled reported having some marital problems relating to money and half of those describe their money problems as significant. Yet, a little thoughtful consideration about money management will go a long way to reducing that strain. Here are several ways for a couple to establish financial fitness.

♥ *Call It Anything but a Budget.* For most people *budget* is the dreaded "B" word because it has negative images of control, deprivation, labor, and struggle. Therefore, many counselors suggest using a more positive word or phrase. "Try calling it a wish list," says Linda Barbanel, a social worker and financial columnist for a newspaper.

One couple, David and Sharon, established a "freedom fund." "We were always in debt, often overdrawn on our checking account and never had savings of any kind," says David. "Then, we decided to set up a plan, but rather than calling it a budget we refer to it as a 'freedom fund.' Included in our financial plan was a mutually agreed systematic savings goal. It's been two years and now we actually have a nice down payment for a condo."

♥ *Have a Financial Plan.* Whatever you call it, do have a financial plan. All professional money managers say budgeting is necessary. "What can you do to get your finances in order?" asks Emily Card, a California attorney and author of several books on personal financing. "To start, stop managing money in your head. A mental budget gives you too much room to rationalize binges and doesn't provide you with an accurate picture of your spending patterns."[2]

Her recommendation is a written and itemized budget listing every income source and expenditure. Every couple should know and understand their financial picture for a full year. This means listing total income (salaries, commissions, bonuses), established expenses (rent, mortgage, car payments, insurance, food), and discretionary spending (entertainment, vacations, personal care). Knowing how much money is coming in and going out is the first step in financial management.

♥ *Leave Room for Fun.* This advice is offered by Judy Lawrence, financial counselor and author of *Common Cents: The Complete Money Management Workbook.* Lawrence cautions against a budget in which pleasure spending is dependent upon leftover money. "You'll end up bickering, frustrated and disappointed with the whole budget idea."[3] She suggests every budget include a line item for "fun" events or purchases such as a yearly vacation, a new CD player, large screen television, etc.

♥ *Hold Regular Financial Meetings.* Every couple should learn to think of their finances as though they were involved in a small family business. Adrian G. Berg, a financial planner and author of *How to Stop Fighting About Money and Make Some*, makes this observation: "When people complain that they can't save, it's often because they administer their home finances so sloppily."[4]

To solve this problem, Berg suggests scheduling regular conferences to discuss money-related issues.

At such meetings, together couples can review income, expenses, and anticipated needs. That would also be the time to re-evaluate financial goals and how best to meet them. Such conferences can also reinforce a couple's commitment to their plans.

♥ *Communicate Openly About Money.* Rather than hide hard feelings about your spouse's spending, it is better to be open about concerns. "If you are having financial problems or think that your mate is being extravagant, say why you don't want him or her to buy a certain item," advise Miriam Arond and Samuel L. Pauker. "Explain your reasoning when you discourage a purchase—that for the price of one expensive sweater you can buy two or three less expensive ones, or that a black dress may lend itself to more uses than a hot-pink dress."[5]

♥ *Establish Common Ground, Not Battle Ground.* Many financial battles can be minimized considerably if couples will establish some common ground rules about spending. Once these guidelines are mutually agreed upon, they should not be violated. Michele Weiner-Davis is a therapist in private practice. While counseling a couple who were constantly blaming each other for their spending habits, Weiner-Davis asked if they had ever had financial disagreements in the previous years of their marriage.

When they said they had, Weiner-Davis asked how they resolved those differences at that time. The wife said: "I guess we just minded our own business. I bought what I wanted to buy. He spent money on different things and I just stayed out of it." In her book, *Divorce Busting,* Weiner-Davis reports making this suggestion to the couple:

I wanted to know whether they thought they could reinstitute a laissez-faire financial policy and they agreed. Since their salaries were considerably higher than in previous years, it increased the possibility of spending large sums of money. Therefore, they added an addendum. If either wanted to purchase an item over a thousand dollars, the spouse had to be consulted. They were extremely pleased with their new old plan.[6]

♥ *Negotiate Individual Differences.* Shortly after Ann, who is a saver, married Don, who is a spender, they found themselves battling over money. In order to break the impasse, Don made a "date" with his wife for dinner where they would try to talk reasonably about their individual financial patterns.

"Amazingly, we came up with a win-win strategy," says Don. "Since I like to spend and she likes to save, we decided to curb any large purchases until we had a secure emergency fund in a savings account. Once we reach that goal, I get to splurge on a purchase that is five hundred dollars or less," Don happily says.

This is a wise couple. By negotiating individual differences each of them gets something of what they want without having to give up what is most important.

Ultimately, money does not need to be the great divider in a marriage. Knowing how to manage money well is a skill everyone can learn. And, mutual money management can be another source of closeness between two people striving for common goals.

[1]Arond and Pauker, *The First Year of Marriage*, p. 158.

[2]Emily Card, cited in "Budgeting: Beat Your Mental Blocks." *Working Woman*, January 1991, p. 38.

[3]Judy Lawrence, *Common Cents: The Complete Money Management Workbook,* cited in Kristin Davis and Bertha Kainen, "Your Family Finances." *Changing Times Magazine*, February 1990, p. 100.

[4]Adrian G. Berg, cited in "How To Beat Money Stress." *Redbook*, May 1991, p. 112.

[5]Arond and Pauker, *The First Year of Marriage*, p. 184.

[6]Michele Weiner-Davis, *Divorce Busting*. Summit Books, 1992, p. 135.

Love is a great thing, a
great good in every wise:
it alone makes light every
heavy thing
and bears evenly every
uneven thing.
　　　—Thomas a Kempis

Committing...

Making Your Marriage "Divorce-proof"

After Frank pulled into the parking lot of the restaurant, he paused before leaving his car. There, he took the time to carefully comb his hair, adjust his tie and look into the mirror for a final check. Stepping out of the car he walked briskly toward the restaurant where he greeted a woman. They embraced, kissed, and held hands together as they made their way inside.

Contrary to appearances this is not a couple who have just started dating, nor are they recently married. They are a husband and wife who have celebrated more than thirty years together. During those years Frank and Grace have enjoyed a husband and wife relationship that has thrived, weathered many storms, and which now continues to bring them both a great deal of satisfaction.

Everyone who falls in love and weds wants the marriage always to be a source of mutual love, joy, and fulfillment. Here are some ties that bind that can "divorce-proof" any marriage.

♥ *Put Each Other First.* This is a key ingredient common to all happily married couples. They do not allow parents or friends or work to be placed ahead of the relationship.

An example is Mike and Pat, who recently renewed wedding vows on their twenty-fifth anniversary. At the reception Mike, who has a thriving and busy dental practice, shared these words with the people present: "The reason Pat and I continue to be so happy together is that we have always placed each other first. When children came along Pat deliberately scheduled a date night alone at least twice a month on our family calendar. In my dental practice, I regularly made an appointment for lunch with Pat."

♥ *Drop the "D" Word.* Women and men who remain fulfilled in their marriages over many years are inevitably those who take seriously the vow, "till death us do part." Divorce is simply not one of their options nor is the term a part of their vocabulary.

Romance writer Nadine Crenshaw, happily married for twenty-three years, offers this personal advice: "Talk about everything—except divorce. There is only one subject we discovered that should be taboo in a marriage: divorce. The mere mention of this word brings it into the realm of possibility." Another couple who feel the same way are Dame Sybil Thorndike, distinguished British actress, and her husband of many decades, Sir Lewis Casson. After his death she was asked about their long and happy marriage: "Did you ever think of divorce?" was one of the questions. Her answer is memorable: "Divorce? Never. But murder often!"[1]

♥ *Keep the Faith.* More and more authorities are saying publicly that people who practice their faith tend to have happier and more stable homes. More is written about this topic in a later chapter, but consider this statement by Brendan McCooey, a circuit court judge in Chicago's Cook County. He presides over domestic violence and divorce cases.

Having observed thousands of couples he says: "There's always something missing. There's a certain spiritual value missing in these families. I don't see anything holding these families together. Any normal crisis in a marriage seems to derail these marriages."[2]

♥ *Deal with Problems Together.* The reality about marriage is that it can be both wonderful and difficult. There will be times of ecstasy as well as times of agony. When there is a difference of opinion and tempers flare it is important to deal with the issue together.

Psychologist and author Ayala Pines interviewed two hundred married couples to determine what happy marriages have in common. High on the list for such couples was the ability to work out problems together.

Dr. Pines writes:

> Happily married women are not only talking to their husbands more, but they're able to discuss any marital problems with their husbands while many unhappily married women are more likely to confide in a friend. By working on problems together, instead of venting your anger elsewhere, you and your husband will learn more about each other and yourselves. Discussing problems in such

a constructive way leads to true intimacy. Never giving each other a chance to probe problems, on the other hand, can only lead to more tension and more unhappiness.[3]

♥ *Laugh Together.* In the book *Intimate Play,* Boston psychiatrist William Betcher identifies play and laughter as crucial ingredients for a happy marriage. "Couples who have fun together are really saying, 'I trust you to love me even when I'm being silly.'"[4]

An example is King Edward VIII, who abdicated the British throne in order to marry the woman he loved, Wallis Warfield Simpson. Addressing a group on the subject of happy marriages, the Duke of Windsor humorously remarked: "Of course, I do have a slight advantage over the rest of you. It helps in a pinch to be able to remind your bride that you gave up a throne for her."

♥ *Accentuate the Positive.* When couples begin to grow apart and become unhappy with each other there is usually a tendency to focus upon their partner's negatives. Constant criticism and faultfinding always drive a wedge between a man and a woman.

On the other hand, happy couples are those who accentuate the positive and focus on the kind, gentle, loving characteristics in their spouse. In her survey, Dr. Pines describes an unhappy woman who is an extreme example of negativity and who actually keeps a "hate book" on her spouse.

"Every time her husband of twelve years does something to annoy or offend her," says Dr. Pines, "she writes it down in her book and says to herself, 'another nail in your coffin.' Whether she realizes it or not, she has spent twelve years training herself to notice only what she dislikes about her husband. How much happier she and her husband—indeed all couples—would be if they put that same energy into relishing what they do like, into keeping, instead, a 'love' book."[5]

♥ *Nurture Love.* Couples who stay in love and remain devoted to each other know how important it is to nurture their love. They never take the relationship for granted nor do they allow themselves to become too tired, too worried, or too busy to be there for each other. Happy couples nurture their love by expressing appreciation, saying "thank you," and offering compliments. They do these things, and more, on a regular basis.

Tracy Cabot, Ph.D., author of *How to Keep a Man in Love with You Forever,* describes one couple she interviewed as the "most shining example of married love." When she spoke with Bob and Alberta they had just celebrated their seventy-third wedding anniversary. They have nine children, nineteen grandchildren, and ten great-grandchildren.

When asked about their long and happy marriage, Alberta said her husband knew how to nurture a relationship. His way was to give flowers accompanied by a tender love letter.

> I'd always find a huge bouquet of flowers on the dresser when I woke up. Bob picked them himself and there was always a note with the flowers. I saved the notes over the years and whenever things were bad and one of the kids was sick or the crops failed, I'd bring out the notes he sent me with the flowers and we'd sit and read them together and we'd always feel better.[6]

Perhaps the best advice for remaining happy as a couple comes from author Jane Wells. Although she lived and wrote earlier in this century, her comments are still valid. She wrote:

> Let your love be stronger than your hate or anger. Learn the wisdom of compromise, for it is better to bend a little than to break. Believe the best rather than the worst. People have a way of living up—or down—to your opinion of them. Remember that true friendship is the basis for any lasting relationship. The person you choose to marry is deserving of the courtesies and kindnesses you bestow on your friends.[7]

[1]Nadine Crenshaw, "How to Find True Love." *Reader's Digest*, May 1991, p. 35.

[2]Brendan McCooey, cited in "Two 'Expert' Dads Judge the State of Modern Fatherhood, Families." *The Daily Herald*, June 16, 1991, p. 1.

[3]Ayala Pines, "What Makes a Couple Happy." *Redbook*, April 1990, p. 102.

[4]William Betcher, cited in Edwin Kiester and Sally Valente Kiester, "Bring Fun Back to Your Marriage." *Reader's Digest*, January 1989, p. 82.

[5]Pines, "What Makes a Couple Happy," p. 102.

[6]Tracy Cabot, *How to Keep a Man in Love with You Forever* McGraw Hill, 1986, p. 235.

[7]Jane Wells, cited in Abigail Van Buren, "Dear Abby." Universal Press Syndicate, July 17, 1987.

Love consists in this, that
two solitudes
protect and border and
salute each other.
　　—Rainer Maria Rilke

8

Differing...
One Love—Two Faiths:
Making the Best of Both Worlds

During the two years that Beth and Roger dated, their families and friends appeared to be supportive and accepting of the relationship. When Roger proposed, Beth was delighted and, of course, accepted his engagement ring.

However, her delight turned to dismay when she informed her parents about their plans for marriage. Beth says: "My mother's reaction will remain permanently etched in my mind. As I spoke of our love and wedding plans, mother's face turned bleach white. She stood up from the sofa, tears flowing down her face, shook her head in strong disapproval and left the room. The relationship with my mother was tense from then on."

The problem for the mother was not a character deficiency in Roger, Beth's fiancé. The issue was one of religion. Roger is Roman Catholic and Beth is Jewish.

Although today's society is much more open about interfaith marriages, these engagements still continue to evoke strong emotions from family and friends.

And, such negative feelings do not only emerge when there is a Jewish-Christian wedding. As a minister, I have witnessed periods of coolness and even hostility within families when an Episcopalian married a Southern Baptist, a Methodist married a Greek Orthodox and when a Lutheran married a Unitarian.

Inevitably, a negative response from family members leaves a couple hurt, confused, and often very angry. Nevertheless, interfaith couples are usually able to weather the initial storm and continue making plans for their wedding and common life together. Here are several simple strategies for happiness and harmony when planning an interfaith marriage.

♥ *Remind Yourself That You Are Not Alone.* At one time couples who married outside of their religious backgrounds were isolated and stigmatized. Today the fact is that interfaith marriages are an increasing reality in the 1990s.

For example, Egon Mayer, professor of sociology at Brooklyn College and author of *Marriage Between Jews and Christians,* notes that in the 1920s the marriage rate between Jews and Christians was less than 2 percent. In the 1960s that figure rose to 15 percent. Today that statistic has grown to nearly 40 percent. In major metropolitan areas as many as 60 percent of couples come from different religious backgrounds.

Consequently, the experience of more and more couples is that a differing religious background does not need to be an impediment to a good marriage.

♥ *Minimize Differences.* Religion is no longer the divisive factor that it was in other decades. Differing religious backgrounds alone should not keep two people in love from marrying. This is the view of Dr. Clara Livesy, a psychiatrist and family therapist.

In her book, *The Marriage Maintenance Manual*, she states: "I think many people get carried away on this point [interfaith marriage]; too much is made of the need to marry someone of the same religious background, especially in the world of today."[1]

A similar outlook is expressed by psychologist Dr. Joyce Brothers, who says, "The negative effect of religious differences on marriage does not seem to be as great as it used to be. It is certainly not the barrier that it often was in times past."[2]

♥ *Maximize Common Ground.* Rather than focus on the religious differences, a healthier approach for a couple is to focus upon similarities. Anthony and Sarah are a good example. Now happily married five years, they recall the cold response from both sets of parents when they announced their engagement. Sarah says:

> Everyone was upset because Tony is Catholic and I am Jewish. However, we decided right away to emphasize what was common in our heritage rather than what could divide us. We were able to win over both sides because in Tony's Catholic Italian background family life is as important as it is for my Jewish relatives. When both sets of families get together it is amazing to see how similar we all are. Both of our families like to serve lots of food and sing until we are all hoarse.

♥ *Have High Hopes.* There will be family members and friends who will say or convey that interfaith marriages "don't have a chance." Balance the pessimistic voices around with a creative and optimistic outlook that you can have an interfaith marriage and be a very happy family.

One of the best books on interfaith marriage is *Happily Intermarried.* The book is written by a rabbi (Roy Rosenberg), a priest (Father Peter Meehan), and a minister (Reverend John Wade Payne). The authors state emphatically that two religions can comfortably co-exist in one home.

> Interreligious families can be found all over. Jews and Christians are marrying each other and having children who grow up to be happy and well adjusted. The prejudices of the past have been forgotten by many today and people more and more are able to relate to one another as individuals, appreciating and respecting one another across religious, ethnic and racial lines.[3]

♥ *Be Patient with Family and Friends.* Remember that an initial negative reaction from a family member is seldom a permanent one. By not giving up a relationship because of family objection, a couple is actually providing the family with time to adjust and accept. Kathy, whose staunch Missouri Synod Lutheran family objected fiercely when she married Mark, a member of the Russian Orthodox church, reports:

> Since my family is a very close one it was hard to resist their pressure to terminate the relationship and call off the marriage. However, Mark and I remained constant in our love and

were married. Now, it's three years later and
my mother has admitted that Mark is her
favorite son-in-law. What a change. I'm glad
we didn't give in!

♥ *Try to Compromise.* One Jewish-Christian couple
found themselves feeling tense and pressured. His parents insisted that they be married by a minister in
their Methodist Church. Her family demanded a temple
wedding performed by their rabbi.

Their solution was a wise one which won the
approval of both families. They were married by both a
minister and a rabbi in the grand ballroom of the
hotel where the reception was held. During the ceremony, the bride stood under a *chuppah,* the traditional Jewish wedding canopy. The minister delivered
a brief nonsectarian sermon on love, an important
topic common to all religions. At the end of the ceremony the groom smashed a glass under his heel,
recalling the destruction of the second Jewish temple
in 70 A.D.

♥ *Participate in Each Other's Religious Life.* Couples
who report satisfying interfaith marriages acknowl-
edge that their partners try to share their dual religious heritage in small but important ways. For example, one Catholic woman who is married to a Jewish man says:

> Before we were married, Dan and I agreed
> that we would take part in each other's im-
> portant holy days. During Christmas Dan
> always joins me for midnight mass at my
> Catholic church. Then, in September, I al-
> ways attend temple services for Yom Kippur
> with him. It's really not much and yet both of

us feel good about sharing and learning more about the other's religious heritage.

Lastly, the large number of interfaith couples are actually a gift to the world. Every successful inter-religious couple who marry, have children, and live in peace and harmony demonstrate how larger religious communities can also do the same. Love is a power that unites men and women across all kinds of social barriers.

[1]Clara Livesy, *The Marriage Maintenance Manual*. Dial Press, 1977, p. 39.

[2]Joyce Brothers, *What Every Woman Ought To Know About Love and Marriage*. Simon & Schuster, 1984, p. 80.

[3]Roy A. Rosenberg, Peter Meehan, and John W. Payne, *Happily Intermarried: Authoritative Advice for a Joyous Jewish-Christian Marriage*. Macmillan Publishing Co., 1989, p. 103.

9

No matter how thoughtfully planned, spoken words frequently come out wrong. A love letter affords the luxury of time, to convey feelings as eloquently as possible.
—Lance Contrucci

Reinforcing...
How to Write the Perfect Love Letter

While sitting in a Paris cafe, Sarah saw an attractive, intriguing man. Immediately, he was someone whom she was determined to meet and win over. Able to arrange an introduction, they quickly fell in love. On one occasion when they had to be apart Sarah wrote this love letter to him.

> Wonderful boy, Where are you tonight? Paris is a morgue without you. Before I knew you, I thought Paris was like heaven but now it is a vast desert of desolation and loneliness....Now I cannot live apart from you—your words dispel all the cares of the world and make me happy. I am as hungry for them as for food. I am thirsty for them and my thirst is over-

whelming. Your words are my food, your breath
my wine. You are everything to me.[1]

That letter was written in the nineteenth century
by French actress Sarah Bernhard to her lover of many
years, Victorien Sardou, a French poet and playwright.
Since then much has changed. The love letter has been
offset by greeting cards, the fax, the telephone answer-
ing machine, and even the telephone itself.

Yet, there is nothing like a love letter to warm the
heart, transform a moment, brighten a day, and leave
a permanent mark. The good news is that you don't
have to be a poet, a Rhodes scholar, or a helpless
romantic to write a love letter. All it takes is your love
for another person and your desire to express your
love. Here are simple ways for anyone to write the
perfect love letter.

♥   *Write from the Heart.* Avoid letting your cerebral
side censor you, saying, "Be careful," "Don't say too
much; you might be sorry." Work to loosen up and
really say how you feel. Martha in Chicago wrote to
her lover in San Francisco while they were tempo-
rarily separated because of a job transfer, saying:

> My dearest David, I am writing you this letter
> for the pure and simple fact that I love you. I
> miss you deeply and want to hear your voice,
> touch your skin, feel you beside me. Tonight,
> look at the Big Dipper and think of me. I will
> do the same for you.

♥   *Be Short.* Shorter is better than longer. Good writing is always characterized by an economy of words.
Keep in mind Mark Twain's advice: "When in doubt,
cross it out." Here is a short love letter (only sixteen

words) that conveys a big message: "I love you—completely, utterly, unshakably, permanently. Hotly, warmly, totally, thoroughly. You are everything to me."

♥ *Be Spontaneous.* Act on your impulses. Spontaneity always has high levels of energy and enthusiasm connected to it. Your words will have a strong effect when you act spontaneously to write a love letter. Consider Rick, an executive away from his wife on business. While flying over the Rocky Mountains he felt inspired to write a love note. Reaching for pen and paper he quickly wrote:

"There is no mountain high enough, no road winding enough, and no valley deep enough to keep me from loving you. I miss you, love you, and can't wait to be with you." He mailed it as soon as his plane landed. Needless to say, his wife was thrilled to receive this spontaneous expression of love.

♥ *Be Original.* Don't slip into easy, overworked clichés. Customize your words for your unique relationship. Who would not love a letter like this one written by Mark in Texas:

Dear Jane, You say you are overweight; I see it as more of you to love. You say your lips are shaped funny; I don't notice that through the warm, sensuous feel of them. You say your feet are too big and wide; I enjoy the extra time it takes to massage every nerve in them. You say we're too poor to enjoy a night on the town; I'd much rather spend the evening holding and loving you.

♥ *Research for Inspiration.* Pick up a book of quotations and include an appropriate statement from a prominent writer. Be sure to credit the author. "When I think of what your love has done for me I am reminded of Elizabeth Barrett Browning's words—"The face of all the world is changed, I think, since I heard the footsteps of thy soul."

Another way to write a love letter is to begin with a quotation followed by your own expression. For example: " 'Love is, above all, the gift of oneself.'—Jean Anoulh. Thank you for sharing and giving yourself to me. I love you."

One man began his note with a thought from French writer Albert Camus. "When I think of our love, I am reminded that Albert Camus identified the 'love of another being' as one of the conditions for happiness. You make me very, very happy. Thank you for loving me for I surely love you."

♥ *Be Sincere.* Sincerity, along with honesty, is fundamental to every loving relationship. When expressing your love in a letter be sincere. This means learning to get in touch with your deepest feelings and expressing them freely.

A good example is Lord Horatio Nelson, Admiral in the British Navy. An order for him to cruise the Mediterranean meant he had to be away from Emma Hamilton, his lover. During their separation he wrote eloquently and painfully how he felt about being away from her. "I am separated from all I hold dear in this world," he told her. Only "the call of our country" could keep them apart, he explained. "No separation...can alter my love and affection for you," he assured Hamilton.[2]

While every spoken expression of love is valued, a love letter is forever. When written it can be read and reread many times, often through several generations.

If Elizabeth Barrett Browning had simply whispered in Robert's ear: "How do I love thee?" her words would have ended that night. Because she took the time to write them, they have warmed the hearts of many people for nearly two centuries.

Even though your love letter may never appear in a book of poetry or quotations, it will touch your mate's heart and soul. In that sense you will indeed have written the perfect love letter.

[1]Sarah Bernhard, *Treasurey of the World's Great Letters*, ed. by M. Lincoln Schuster. Simon & Schuster, 1940, p. 371.
[2]Lord Horatio Nelson, *The Faber Book of Letters*, ed. by Felix Pryor. Faber & Faber, 1988, p. 90f.

Not Truth, but Faith, it is
that keeps the world alive.
—Edna St. Vincent Millay

10

Anchoring...
Keeping the Faith as a Family

Over a ten-year period, three thousand families were studied to discover what made their family life strong and rewarding. Common to the families interviewed was the vital importance of a spiritual center.

In the book that resulted from the study, *Secrets of Strong Families,* authors Nick Stinnett and John DeFrain, both professors of family studies at the University of Nebraska, state:

> Over and over again the strong families talked about an unseen power that *can* change lives, *can* give strength to endure the hardest times, *can* provide hope and purpose....Spiritual wellness is illustrated by our strong families

as a unifying force, a caring center within each person that promotes sharing, love and compassion for others. It is a force that helps a person transcend self and become part of something larger.[1]

Like the authors of this study, the writers of scripture recognized the importance of a spiritual center for strong and healthy family life. In Psalm 84 we read: "Happy are those who live in your house....They go from strength to strength."

While most couples and families welcome opportunities for spiritual awareness and growth, many don't take the time to intentionally plan for it. Here are seven strategies to keep the faith as a family and thereby be in touch with a powerful, important source of insight and strength.

♥ *Surround Yourself with Christian Friends.* Keeping company with others who share your values and perspectives will go a long way toward solidifying a spiritual tone in the home.

Kevin and Marilyn Ryan, authors of *Making a Marriage,* share this personal awareness from their own family life:

> Though we have friends of many stripes and religious views, ranging from highly committed to openly antagonistic, we believe it's important to have a core of religious friends. Quite frankly, we need their example and support. They remind us of how we should be thinking and how we should be living. For most people this can be achieved by being involved with a group of people in one's church.[2]

♥ *Attend Worship Regularly.* "I don't believe in organized religion," was a statement made to Rabbi Harold Kushner by a young man. In his book *Who Needs God?,* Rabbi Kushner shares his response: "He and I spoke for about an hour. I told him that some people can create lives of holiness all by themselves, the way Mozart could create immortal music without taking piano lessons, but that most of us need a structure and the company of other people to do it."[3]

Of course, Rabbi Kushner is right. It is nearly impossible to have a spiritual center if we do not attend consistently a place where religious truth is taught. Also, learning and growing is made easier in the company of other people who are striving for similar goals. It is worth noting that in the gospels Jesus is reported as attending synagogue worship regularly.

♥ *Tune in to the Service.* There is no value in being physically present for worship but intellectually absent. As the service begins, work at being involved in every aspect: pray the prayers, listen to the sermon, sing from your heart, hear the announcements about the faith community.

One couple have a creative response to sermons that come across as dull or difficult to understand. "My husband and I decided we would take notes when the pastor began his sermon. He is very gifted intellectually and we found ourselves often not concentrating properly. Taking notes helps us focus. After the service and over lunch we talk about the sermon to further clarify and make applications for our living in the week to come."

♥ *Get Involved in the Faith Community.* While some people just drop in and out once a week, most individuals find they benefit much more by additional involvement in the church. It is the difference between being a religious spectator and a participant.

Find a way to make your spiritual commitment more concrete by participating in a midweek Bible study, attending a retreat, singing in the choir, visiting the sick and shut-in, or teaching a class. Congregations become more vibrant Christian communities when everyone actively participates.

♥ *Kick the Bunny Out of Easter.* Try shifting the focus from the secular and commercial aspects to the original spiritual reasons for the seasons. Observe the church year as a family by accentuating Christian celebrations.

Kevin and Marilyn Ryan feel strongly about recapturing the church year. "Kick the bunny out of Easter," they write. "Religious holidays like Christmas, Easter and Thanksgiving have been smothered by cloying commercialism. We have to wake ourselves up consciously to the fact that amid all of the Christmas madness, the cards, shopping and assembling of toys, some mystery is going on."[4]

Christmas, for example, is an ideal time to acquaint children with the story of Nicholas. This godly man was an early church leader with a special compassion for needy children. The Santa Claus myth is derived from the life of Nicholas. Most public and church libraries have excellent books on Nicholas that can be read to children.

♥ *Pray Regularly.* While the next chapter deals more completely with the topic of prayer, here I would simply encourage every couple to cultivate the habit of regularly thinking in the presence of God. Beyond prayers offered in a worship service, set aside some time, preferably daily, to spend in meditation and prayer. These moments will not only keep you more connected to God but will be a fruitful time of growth and guidance. Rev. Norman Vincent Peale, in his book *A Guide to Confident Living*, observes:

> People who practice the simple techniques of prayer secure guidance to an unusual degree. They are directed in their activities and contacts by an invisible but definite power. In meeting situations and in dealing with people they acquire remarkable skill. I do not, of course, believe there is anything magical in prayer, but from my experience I do feel certain that insights, leads and illuminations are given to people who habitually practice an attitude of prayer.[5]

♥ *Have Family Devotions.* It is true that the family that prays together, stays together. DeFrain and Stinnett suggest: "Read Bible stories or other inspirational material, pray, sing, count your blessings, reaffirm your love and commitment to each other. Keep devotionals short and varied so that the interest of children is stimulated rather than squelched."[6]

Always remember that Jesus taught, "If you have faith the size of a mustard seed, you will say to this mountain, 'Move from here to there,' and it will move" (Matthew 17:20). Families who keep the faith find they have a resilience and a power to move mountains by overcoming obstacles and transforming tragedies into triumphs.

[1]Stinnett and DeFrain, *Secrets of Strong Families*, p. 100.

[2]Ryan and Ryan, *Making a Marriage*, p. 201.

[3]Harold Kushner, *Who Needs God?*   Summit Books, 1989, p. 16.

[4]Ryan and Ryan, *Making a Marriage*, p. 202.

[5]Norman Vincent Peale, *A Guide to Confident Living.* Prentice Hall, 1948, p. 106.

[6]Stinnett and DeFrain, *Secrets of Strong Families*, p. 100.

11

Prayer is the
contemplation of the
facts of life from the
highest point of view.
—Ralph Waldo Emerson

Praying...
The Importance of a
Spiritual Center

An important form of intimacy is prayer. Love and prayer are two sides of the same coin. Couples who pray together, for each other, and over common concerns have one more powerful bond for their marriage and friendship. Minister and author Norman Vincent Peale makes this important observation:

> Although this sounds like standard preacher's advice, don't dismiss it too easily. I can't guarantee that every family that prays together stays together. But, I can tell you that in all my years of counseling, I have never encountered a couple in serious difficulty who were praying together. Nor have I ever known a couple who, once they had agreed to pray

together, and stuck to it, wound up by getting a divorce.[1]

Poet Alfred Lord Tennyson wrote this about the importance of prayer: "More things are wrought by prayer than this world dreams of. Wherefore, let thy voice rise like a fountain." Like Tennyson, Paul also emphasized the significance of prayer. Repeatedly Paul states: "Devote yourselves to prayer" (Colossians 4:2). "Persevere in prayer" (Romans 12:12).

Then there is the example of Jesus, who is recorded in the Gospels as constantly withdrawing for times of prayer during his ministry.

While every Christian would agree with Tennyson, Paul, Jesus, and Rev. Peale on the fact that prayer is an indispensable aspect of Christian living, many couples struggle with the issue of making time for prayer. In a busy, frenzied day, where can Christians make room for prayer and meditation? Here are several practical suggestions for incorporating prayer into daily living without adding to an already overcrowded schedule.

♥ *Pray While Waiting in Lines.* The word "wait" appears often in scripture. Psalm 37:7 is one example: "Be still before the LORD, and wait patiently for him." An ideal time to offer prayers and wait for God, so to speak, can be while standing in lines at the grocery store or the post office.

On one occasion, I found myself in a painfully long and slow line at the bank. I became quite impatient and then decided to make use of the time by praying for various people I knew who had pressing needs. As I prayed I immediately became aware of a banker weeping quietly at her desk.

Leaving my place in line, I made my way to her. I simply stated that I could see she was upset and wondered if I could help. She asked me to be seated and told me that day was the first anniversary of her college-aged son's death. He had died from leukemia one year earlier. She talked and I listened for a few minutes. When she was through the woman thanked me repeatedly for allowing her to share her sadness, telling me she felt "much better" because of our conversation.

♥ *Try the Five-finger Exercise.* Some Christians become frustrated by the fact that their prayers include some but neglect others. One way to be more comprehensive and consistent in prayer is to try the five-finger exercise.

This concept is recommended by Dr. William Barclay, author of many religious books. Dr. Barclay tells of a nurse who used her hands as a scheme for prayer. In his commentary on the book of Philippians, he explains:

> Each finger stood for someone. Her thumb was nearest to her and it reminded her to pray for those who were closest to her. The second finger was used for pointing and it stood for all her teachers in school and in the hospital. The third finger was the tallest and it stood for the V. I. P.s, the leaders in every sphere of life. The fourth finger was the weakest, as every pianist knows, and it stood for those who were in trouble and in pain. The little finger was the smallest and the least important to the nurse. It stood for herself.[2]

♥ *Light a Candle.* Light is a biblical image for the presence and power of God. Psalm 27:1 states: "The LORD is my light and my salvation." An effective way to make use of this symbol is to light a candle in your home as reminder to pray for God's presence and power in someone's life.

This is something we do regularly in our household. We have placed candles strategically in various rooms. Whenever we learn about someone who needs immediate and constant prayer, we light those candles. That way, no matter where we move in the house, we see a lit candle and offer a brief prayer for that individual.

This week, for example, we have lit candles for a friend who will have a baby on Friday. Her pregnancy has become somewhat complicated and she will have a cesarean section. The candles remind us of Laura and her situation. We offer prayers for Laura and her child.

♥ *Use the Brother Lawrence Approach.* Brother Lawrence was a 17th century lay member of the Carmelite order. Upon entering the monastery he was assigned to work in the kitchen. The great contribution of this mystic was his blending of manual labor with prayer. It was in the kitchen where he prayed most often.

His approach is applicable for today. Most people have times of labor when the body is working but the mind is not. For example, one man offers prayers as he mows his lawn. Another man prays while he is refinishing furniture. And a woman speaks to God about various needs while she washes, folds, and irons clothing for her family of seven.

♥ *Make Use of "Down" Time.* One woman, herself a busy mother of three and a public relations director for a large corporation, says she "salvaged" her prayer life when she realized she had almost two hours daily while commuting to and from work.

> I almost gave up regular prayer because my schedule was so overcrowded. Then I began to use the time driving to and from my office. It's actually the perfect time to pray and meditate. There are no interruptions at all. No kids calling for me and there is no telephone ringing. What I do is use the morning time to pray. When I'm on my way home I listen to religious tapes and music.

♥ *Pray Your Appointment Book.* Almost everyone keeps a daily calendar of some kind that records meetings, doctor's appointments, and conferences. Ron, a friend of mine who is an attorney, uses his lunch hour for this purpose.

"Three years ago," he says, "I realized my law practice had grown so rapidly that it left me with very little discretionary time. Rather than give up daily prayer I decided to pray during the thirty minutes I use for lunch. There, I pray for people and events that are recorded in my appointment book for the day. That has included my clients, my children on field trips, teachers conferences, and church meetings."

No one should ever give up cultivating a prayer life because they miss a day periodically. Here is a helpful example from the life of Cardinal Francis Spellman, for many years the archbishop of New York. A weary and overworked executive once asked the Cardinal, "With all the work you do, do you ever get so tired that you forget to say your prayers at night?"

Cardinal Spellman replied: "When I'm so tired and I can't keep my eyes open, I simply say, 'Dear God, you know I've been working in your vineyard all day. If you don't mind, could we skip the details till morning?"

While these suggestions are certainly not exhaustive, using them allows even the busiest couple to make their life a prayer. Also these methods are a way to apply the teaching of Paul, who invites all Christians to "pray constantly" (1 Thessalonians 5:17).

[1]Norman Vincent Peale, "A First Aid Kit for Marriage." *Plus*, July/August 1989, p. 18.

[2]William Barclay, *The Daily Study Bible: The Letters to the Philippians, Colossians and Thessalonians*. G.R. Welch and Company, 1956, p. 14.

Appendix:

Prayers for God's Blessings on Marriage and Family Life

For Mutual Love and Support

Eternal God . . .
>Look with favor upon this man
>>and this woman whom you make
>>one flesh in Holy Matrimony.

Grant them wisdom and devotion
>in the ordering of their
>>common life,
>that each may be to the other
>>a strength in need,
>>a counselor in perplexity,
>>a comfort in sorrow,
>>and a companion in joy.

Grant that their wills may be
    so knit together in your will,
        and their spirits in your Spirit,
        that they may grow in love and peace
        with you and one another
        all the days of their life.

Give them grace, when they hurt each other,
    to recognize and acknowledge their fault and to
        seek each other's forgiveness
        and yours.

Give them such fulfillment of their
    mutual affection that they
        may reach out in love
        and concern for others.
                —Episcopal Book of Common Prayer

To Be Free of Pettiness

Keep us, O God, from all pettiness.
Let us be large in thought,
    in word, in deed.
Let us be done with faultfinding
    and leave off all self-seeking.
May we put away all pretense
    and meet each other face to face,
    without self-pity,
    and without prejudice.
May we never be hasty in judgment,
    and always generous.
Let us always take time for all things,
    and make us grow calm, serene, gentle.

Teach us to put into action
    our better impulses,
    to be straightforward and unafraid.
Grant that we may realize
    that it is the little things
    of life that create differences,
    that in the big things of life
    we are as one.
And, O Lord God,
    let us not forget to be kind!
      —Queen Mary Stuart (1542–1587)

For a Pure Heart

Lord, grant me a holy heart
    that sees always what is fine
    and pure
    and is not frightened at the sight of sin,
      but creates order wherever it goes.
Grant me a heart that knows nothing
    of boredom, weeping and sighing.
Let me not be too concerned with
    the bothersome thing I call "myself."
Lord, give me a sense of humor
    and I will find happiness in life
    and profit for others.
        —Sir Thomas More (1478–1535)

For Help with Life's Burdens

God of our life, there are days
    when the burdens we carry
    chafe our shoulders and weight us down;
    when the road seems dreary and endless,
    the skies grey and threatening;
        when our lives have no music in them,
        and our hearts are lonely,
        and our souls have lost courage.
Flood the path with light,
    turn our eyes to where the skies
    are full of promise;
        tune our hearts to brave music;
        give us the sense of comradeship with heroes
        and saints of every age;
        and so quicken our spirits
        that we may be able to encourage
        the souls of all who journey with us
        on the road of life, to your honor and glory.
                —Augustine (354–430)

To Be One in the Spirit

God the Father,
    origin of all that is divine,
    good beyond all that is good,
    fair beyond all that is fair,
        in you is calmness,
                peace,
                and concord.

Heal what divides us from one another
    and bring us back into the unity of love, bearing
    some likeness to your divine nature.
Through the embrace of love
    and the bonds of godly affection,
    make us one in the Spirit
    by your peace that makes
        all things peaceful.
We ask this through the grace,
                mercy,
                and tenderness
of your only begotten Son,
    Jesus Christ, our Lord.
                —Dionysius of Alexandria (200–264)

For Forgiveness

Most merciful God,
    we confess that we have sinned
        against you in thought,
                word,
                and deed,
    by what we have done
    and by what we have left undone.
We have not loved you with our whole heart;
    we have not loved our neighbors as ourselves.
We are truly sorry and we humbly repent. For the
sake of your son Jesus Christ
        have mercy on us and forgive us;
        that we may delight in your will,
        and walk in your ways,
        to the glory of your name. Amen.
          —Episcopal Book of Common Prayer

For Divine Assistance

May the strength of God guide me this day
    and may his power preserve me.
May the wisdom of God instruct me;
        the eye of God watch over me;
        the ear of God hear me;
        the word of God give sweetness
            to my speech;
        the hand of God defend me;
        and may I follow the way of God.
Christ be with me, Christ before me,
Christ be after me, Christ within me,
Christ beneath me, Christ above me,
Christ at my right hand, Christ at my left
Christ in the fort, Christ in the chariot,
Christ in the ship,
Christ in the heart of every man
        who thinks of me,
Christ in the mouth of every man
        who speaks to me.
Christ in every eye that sees me.
Christ in every ear that hears me.
                —St. Patrick (390–460)